METAL

COCKTAILS

MARC
AUMONT

FABIEN
LABBÉ

METAL
COCKTAILS
42 RECIPES

Inspired by the World's Biggest Bands

PHOTOGRAPHY
**NICOLAS
LOBBESTAEL**

GRAPHICS
**JULIEN
HENRY**

STYLING
**MÉLANIE
MARTIN**

CONTENTS

Saint-Brieuc, France
January 14, 2022

AN UNEXPECTED JOURNEY

This is a tale of two worlds colliding. It's a multisensory big bang ready to take you on a journey. It's a story of two worlds, distant yet connected: mixology and heavy metal music. Your journey can begin from either side. You can learn about mixology by retracing the grand history of heavy metal, or you can explore the fascinating world of extreme music and its icons through a variety of original recipes. The choice is yours. Follow the legends that have forged the cult of metal straight to your new favorite recipe, or let a cocktail that sounds good set the playlist for your next party!

To keep both of these paths open for you, we have created every recipe to meet two requirements. Each one not only offers inspiration and the knowledge you need to begin mixing your own cocktails, but it also pays tribute to a current of music that was born underground and now runs through all of pop culture.

This book was designed to be an immersive experience for all your senses. So throw on an album and get busy behind the bar! Enjoy the opportunity to taste ingredients from far-flung places, and experience the way a bitter undertone or a bracing touch of acid can take a drink to the next level—the tasting equivalent to getting hooked by a solid thrash metal riff.

Follow our recipes step by step, measure carefully, taste everything, and find the right balance. We've tinkered with the sweetness, acidity, temperature, and texture of each drink, but in the end, you're the bartender! We encourage you to keep adjusting our recipes until they taste just the way you like them.

These days, we're fortunate to have access to high-quality ingredients, so take advantage of the best of the season. You can garnish your daiquiri with strawberries in July and kiwis in December—and you can listen to Josh Homme's desert sessions in the summer while saving Behemoth's icy black metal for winter!

Speaking of ice, here's a bartender's tip: *Never* skimp on the ice. Despite what you may have heard, the colder your cocktail is and the more ice there is in the glass, the slower it will melt and, thus, the less your drink will be diluted.

As you explore these pages, we hope you enjoy the journey through two fascinating worlds that, you will soon see, are a perfect pairing. Refine your presentation and service. Pour your heart into your drinks. The smiles on the lips of your guests when they take their first sips will be your reward.

Bottoms up!

FABIEN & MARC

MARC AUMONT

Marc Aumont is a journalist who loves music, especially metal. He's also a musician who has been playing bass for 24 years in various grindcore, electro, and post-punk bands.

He has published many books with Plon, Hachette Pratique, and Hachette Heroes. As a pop culture specialist, Aumont is fascinated by heavy metal music, the culture that has grown up around it, and the phenomenon of a genre that was born underground but now feeds so broadly into our collective imagination.

FABIEN LABBÉ

A mixologist who studied the craft with Yves Cosentino, Fabien Labbé is a bartender and the owner of Le Bistrot de la Poste in Saint-Brieuc, in Brittany. This watering hole attracts a diverse crowd of musicians, shopkeepers, young people and families, sports fans, the elderly, penniless patrons, and prominent local figures.

Labbé's involvement in the Binic Folks Blues Festival keeps him connected to his passion for rock music. He never stops working and is constantly expanding his knowledge of spirits, cocktails, and bar culture in general. His aim: using high-quality ingredients to create delicious cocktails that get people talking.

GETTING READY

MIXOLOGY GLOSSARY

DASH

A dash is about ⅛ teaspoon of a liquid, generally bitters. You can use a dash bottle to measure out this drop.

DASH BOTTLE

A small bottle that generally contains bitters.

DOUBLE STRAIN

Strain a cocktail with a standard strainer and then again with a fine strainer.

DRY SHAKE

Shake without ice, often to emulsify a cocktail.

EXPRESS CITRUS ZEST

With a peeler, remove a strip of citrus zest. Twist the zest over the glass to squeeze out as much of the essential oil as possible. You can also rub the edges of the glass with the zest because that is where the lips will touch first.

SUGAR CUBE

A sugar cube contains about 1 teaspoon granulated sugar, and it earns you style points.

CHILL A GLASS

Prepare a glass to hold a cocktail, either by putting it in the freezer or by filling it with ice.

REVERSE DRY SHAKE

Shake the cocktail with ice to chill it, and then shake again without ice to emulsify.

SHAKER

Mix a cocktail using a shaker.

SIROP SIMPLE

Simple syrup is easy to make and tastes much better than any cane syrup you can buy at a store. Place equal parts water and sugar (for example, ½ cup water and ½ cup sugar makes about ¾ cup simple syrup) in a saucepan over medium heat. Stir until the sugar is dissolved. Remove from heat.

TOP

Sometimes we finish a cocktail by adding a small pour of sparkling water, tonic, or other soda. We call this "topping" the cocktail.

TOOLS AND GLASSWARE

To mix the perfect drink, a bartender needs a few special tools beyond the run-of-the-mill kitchen utensils. Here's a quick overview of some tools you'll need to begin making our cocktails.

BASIC TOOLS

BOSTON SHAKER

This style of shaker is the go-to for bartenders around the world, and it's the one we recommend you get. It's made of two metal tins, it's easy to handle, and it's much easier to clean than a three-piece shaker with a built-in strainer.

BAR SPOON

Essential for mixing your cocktails and stacking ingredients.

MIXING GLASS

Helpful for mixing cold ingredients. Choosing one with a pour spout makes it easier to transfer your concoctions into the serving glass.

COCKTAIL STRAINER

You'll need this to strain out any solids (like fruit or ice) when you're done shaking your drink. Opt for a Hawthorne strainer, which fits any glass.

FINE STRAINER

When used with a cocktail strainer, a fine strainer removes smaller ingredients such as herbs and fruit pulp.

JIGGER

A bartender's most important liquid measuring tool. It has two sides with different capacities (often ¾ ounce and 1½ ounces in the US, and 20 mL and 40 mL elsewhere). To use, hold the jigger between your middle and index fingers.

MUDDLER

Easily crush citrus and other fruit with a muddler.

CHANNEL KNIFE

Although you can certainly use a vegetable peeler, a channel knife helps you more easily cut consistent strips of zest.

LIQUID CONVERSIONS

Here's a quick guide for measuring our recipes in ounces: 30 mL = 1 ounce. (10 mL = ⅓ ounce. 15 mL = ½ ounce.)

GLASSWARE

OLD FASHIONED GLASS

An absolute must-have! This simple shape is used for many cocktails. Its thick base makes ice last longer because the glass warms more slowly in the hand. When we call for an old fashioned glass in this book, we mean the larger size of this classic: a double old fashioned glass.

HIGHBALL GLASS

The large capacity of this glass makes it perfect for long drinks, which are served with tonic or soda.

COUPE GLASS

This glass has a small capacity and is ideal for cocktails served without ice.

MULE MUG

The signature mug for serving the iconic Moscow Mule.

SHOT GLASS

A shot glass is a small glass (around 1½ ounces in the US, 30 mL to 50 mL elsewhere) designed to hold liquor or a "shooter" cocktail. The contents are usually swallowed in one gulp.

WINE GLASS

Perfect for a spritz or a gin and tonic, the wine glass can be used for a variety of cocktails.

JULEP CUP

A cup made of silver helps keep drinks cold. This one is used mainly to serve Julep-style cocktails.

METAL STORIES

To toast one of the funniest recorded falls in the entire history of metal, we devised this advanced cocktail that features a tower of foam rising out of the glass, like an ice geyser in an Abbath music video.

ABBATH THE MAGNIFICENT

It was 2017, at the popular MetalDays festival in Slovenia. A few audience members had their cell phones out, perhaps sensing that something spectacular was about to go down. The horn and trumpet blasts of the concert's bombastic opening were already exploding out of the enormous speakers when Abbath himself climbed up the hill where the audience was sitting, in full makeup and covered in studs from head to toe. After riling up the crowd for a while, he began an ill-fated charge back down the hill. Guitar strapped on and ready to play, he rushed toward the stage to shouts of encouragement from the front rows . . . and then tripped and faceplanted in a clash of metal strings.

Fall from hell

INGREDIENTS

- 50 mL aquavit
- 20 mL vanilla syrup
- 25 mL lemon juice
- 40 mL heavy whipping cream
- 1 drop orange blossom water
- 1 egg white (or 15 mL aquafaba)
- Sparkling water

TOOLS

- Shaker
- Highball glass
- Straw

DIRECTIONS

1. Pour the aquavit, vanilla syrup, lemon juice, heavy whipping cream, and orange blossom water into a shaker.

2. Shake vigorously with 5 ice cubes for 30 seconds to chill the cocktail.

3. Strain, discard the ice, and add the egg white.

4. Now shake without ice (reverse dry shake) for another 2 minutes while headbanging.

5. Immediately pour the cocktail into a chilled glass. Put the drink in the freezer for about 2 minutes.

6. Poke a hole into the center of the drink with a straw, and then pour in the sparkling water. Like an iceberg, the foam will rise up out of the glass!

Henry Carl Ramos made a name for himself in late-nineteenth-century New Orleans with this foam that floats up out of the glass. He employed as many as 35 bartenders to take turns shaking his cocktails for 10 minutes each.

Ozzy Osbourne will always belong in the pantheon of metal gods. The former lead vocalist for Black Sabbath, who has been doing his thing like no one else for more than 60 years, is probably the only person ever to have taken a bite out of a bat in a live concert. Huge respect, huge shooter.

IT TASTED ALL CRUNCHY AND WARM

On January 20, 1982, Ozzy Osbourne was playing the Veterans Memorial Auditorium in Des Moines, Iowa. In the middle of the concert, a fan threw a bat up onto the stage. Ozzy, who loves to be provocative and never misses a chance to shock, grabbed what he thought was a plastic toy and bit into it with an infernal snarl. But what poor Ozzy didn't realize was that the animal had just been stunned after being tossed onto the stage. It was very much real . . . and alive! The moment the vocalist's teeth sank into the critter, it revived and began to struggle and flap its wings while Ozzy was trying to get it out of his mouth. "I put it in my mouth as a joke. Its wings started flapping and I ripped it out of my mouth, but its head came off! It tasted all crunchy and warm, like a Ronald McDonald's," he said afterward. Stories don't get much more metal than that, and this one clearly deserves a bat brain shooter.

bat SABBATH

INGREDIENTS

✤ 30 mL vodka

✤ 10 mL strawberry syrup

✤ 10 mL Baileys

TOOLS

✤ Shot glass

DIRECTIONS

1. Pour the vodka and strawberry syrup into the shot glass, and stir.

2. Carefully pour in the Baileys, and let the bat brain form in the center of the glass.

3. Swallow in a single gulp.

Have you ever wondered why on earth Guns N' Roses chose a close-up of an ordinary plate of spaghetti as the cover art for the band's fifth album? And what does the title of that album refer to? Better ask the bartender . . .

PASS THE PARMESAN

In the early 1990s, the American supergroup was the living embodiment of hard rock: marathon tours, enormous concerts, endless shenanigans . . . and run-ins with the law. It wasn't until years after the band released *The Spaghetti Incident?* that bassist Duff McKagan finally told the real story behind the album's name. Former drummer Steven Adler, who had been fired for drug use, used to keep his cocaine in the fridge between containers of takeout Italian food. When Adler sued the band, a trial lawyer asked McKagan to tell the court about "the spaghetti incident" that the band members kept referring to. The phrase struck McKagan as so ludicrous that it came to mind when it was time to name the new album.

GIN N' ROSES

INGREDIENTS

- 1 whole bell pepper
- 50 mL celery-infused gin
- 120 mL tomato juice
- 10 mL lemon juice
- ½ teaspoon soy sauce
- Tabasco
- 1 celery stalk
- 1 lemon round

TOOLS

- Mixing glass

DIRECTIONS

1. Prepare the bell pepper "cup" by slicing off the top of the pepper and carefully cleaning out the insides.

2. Pour the gin, tomato juice, and lemon juice into a mixing glass.

3. Season to taste with soy sauce and Tabasco. Stir with 8 ice cubes.

4. Pour the cocktail and ice into the bell pepper. Add a celery stick and a lemon round.

5. Set the pepper in the middle of a plate of spaghetti topped with tomato sauce.

CELERY-INFUSED GIN

There's nothing like a simple infusion to add flavors to a spirit. All you have to do is steep any ingredient in alcohol for a certain amount of time. In this case, drop a celery stick into a bottle of gin, and leave it for 24 hours. Strain and then use!

Following a drug overdose, bassist Nikki Sixx of the notorious Mötley Crüe was pronounced clinically dead for several minutes. Competing stories circulate about what brought him back to life—now we can add this cocktail to the list.

In the mid-1980s, Nikki Sixx and his Mötley Crüe bandmates were taking the world by storm, spreading their gospel of hard rock for the masses with bravado, tight leather pants, and hits that came at you like a truck driver on speed. The band was living the rock star lifestyle, and its members were well known at the time for using and abusing all kinds of drugs. On December 23, 1987, it looked like Nikki had finally taken way too much. He was pronounced dead and stayed that way for several long minutes. According to his own story, the paramedics saved him with a shot of adrenaline to the heart. Steven Adler (of Guns N' Roses), however, claims to have revived him by dragging him into the shower and slapping him in the face. Yet another version tells that Slash's girlfriend brought Nikki back to life by giving him mouth-to-mouth. If you ask us, this shooter definitely would have done the trick.

KICKSTART my HEART

INGREDIENTS

- 1 teaspoon ground coffee
- 1 teaspoon granulated sugar
- 30 mL vodka
- 1 orange wedge

TOOLS

- Shot glass

DIRECTIONS

1. Stir together the coffee and sugar in a container.

2. Pour the vodka into a shot glass.

3. Place the orange wedge next to the vodka.

4. Swallow a heaping spoonful of caffeinated sugar, down the vodka shot, and then take a big bite out of the orange wedge.

5. Call back 911, and tell them to cancel the ambulance.

ICONS

The Old Fashioned may well be the most iconic cocktail of all time. It gets an update here in honor of the greatest metal superstar of all time: Lemmy Kilmister, the late, lamented founder of Motörhead, whose drink of choice was always a Jack and Coke.

A LONG RELATIONSHIP

The love story between Lemmy and Jack Daniel's lasted for decades. The Tennessee whiskey was officially listed in Motörhead's rider,* and the famous square bottle appeared in the background of many an interview with the band's frontman. The two even made it official when the whiskey brand released the Motörhead Limited Edition: Jack Daniel's Single Barrel Select. That one-time batch was sold out in a matter of hours.

LEMMY
Old FASHIONED

INGREDIENTS

- 15 mL cola syrup
- 12 dashes Angostura bitters
- 150 mL Jack Daniel's
- 1 strip orange zest
- 1 maraschino cherry

TOOLS

- Old fashioned glass
- Bar spoon

DIRECTIONS

1. Pour the cola syrup and bitters into the glass.

2. Mix with 1 ice cube using a bar spoon.

3. Pour in the Jack Daniel's. Add a second ice cube, and stir again with the bar spoon.

4. Express a strip of orange zest, and add it to the glass along with the maraschino cherry.

5. Raise your glass to Lemmy, and enjoy your drink to the sounds of *Ace of Spades*.

COLA SYRUP

Purchase a high-quality organic cola, and cook it in a saucepan over low heat to reduce it by half. Let cool.

An artist's list of items that must be provided in their dressing room

To fans of the genre, the legendary metal martyr Dead epitomized the terrifying essence of black metal right up to his tragic death.

Before his grim and premature death by suicide in 1991, Per Yngve Ohlin (his real name) and Norwegian band Mayhem invented a dark, toxic, ultraviolent, and terribly disturbing strain of black metal. The vocalist would descend into horrors even before a concert began: Legend has it he would bury his stage costumes for several days before a show; then to fully enter into his character as an extreme frontman, Dead would inhale the fumes of a dead crow that he kept in a plastic bag just before striding out onto the stage. This pallid cocktail honors the memory of a young man who devoted his short life to trve black metal.

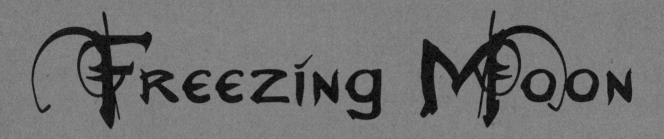

FREEZING MOON

INGREDIENTS

- 50 mL vodka
- 25 mL Algebra Coffee Liqueur
- 30 mL heavy whipping cream
- 15 mL Baileys

TOOLS

- Old fashioned glass
- Shaker

DIRECTIONS

1. Fill an old fashioned glass with ice cubes. Add the vodka and coffee liqueur.

2. Pour the cream, the Baileys, and 1 ice cube into a shaker. Shake vigorously.

3. Delicately pour the cream into the old fashioned glass so that it floats on top.

Although it was first served in the 1960s, the White Russian, which is the inspiration for our Freezing Moon, exploded in popularity after *The Big Lebowski,* during which the Dude drinks no fewer than nine of the now-iconic cocktails.

Latino guitarist Dino Cazares deserves his own special cocktail that features—of course—a glassful of tequila, along with an adventurous smoking technique to reflect his innovative and slightly provocative musical career.

Born in California in 1966, Dino is best known as the founding member and star guitarist of industrial metal band Fear Factory. His specialty is an idiosyncratic technique that makes each riff he plays sound like a round from a machine gun, matched in surgically precise rhythm to the sounds of the double bass drum. The result is an instantly identifiable style that jumps out at you from the first bars of *Demanufacture*, the group's most influential album. Dino thrives on provocation. On top of inventing his own unique style, he has also played with grindcore supergroup Brujeria, which boasts Latino gang masks, ultrapolitical lyrics, rebellion, terrorism, and calls for uprising. Pancho Villa would be proud. This cocktail was inspired by the famous Tequila Sunrise, but with a heretical twist that combines smoke and fresh grapefruit.

LA MIGRA PALOMA

INGREDIENTS

- 2 sprigs rosemary
- 1 fresh grapefruit
- 1 lime, cut into wedges
- 50 mL tequila
- 10 mL agave syrup
- Pinch of salt
- 30 mL sparkling water

TOOLS

- Highball glass
- Shaker

DIRECTIONS

1. Light a sprig of rosemary on fire, and snuff it out by placing the highball glass upside down over the sprig.

2. Cut a strip of zest from the grapefruit. Juice the grapefruit, and strain out the pulp. Set aside 80 mL (⅓ cup) of the juice.

3. Set aside 1 wedge of lime, for garnish. Squeeze the other wedges until you have 10 mL lime juice.

4. Pour the grapefruit juice, tequila, agave syrup, salt, and lime juice into a shaker. Shake.

5. Fill the highball glass with ice cubes, pour the cocktail over the ice, and then top with sparkling water.

6. Stir, express a grapefruit zest into the drink, and garnish with a sprig of rosemary and a lime wedge.

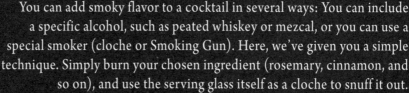

BARTENDER'S TIP

You can add smoky flavor to a cocktail in several ways: You can include a specific alcohol, such as peated whiskey or mezcal, or you can use a special smoker (cloche or Smoking Gun). Here, we've given you a simple technique. Simply burn your chosen ingredient (rosemary, cinnamon, and so on), and use the serving glass itself as a cloche to snuff it out.

I dolized by some and derided by others, Dave Mustaine is a polarizing force. The former Metallica guitarist was fired in the mid-1980s during the group's meteoric rise, and he never forgave bandmates Hetfield and Ulrich: He nursed a grudge for decades. Such a thwarted destiny calls for an equally bitter cocktail.

Of course, it's true that Mustaine committed indiscretions of every sort during his time with Metallica: He drank staggering quantities of alcohol, sowed chaos onstage, played the diva, pulled drunken pranks that ended badly, and more. Metallica's patience finally wore out in 1983, when Mustaine was unceremoniously kicked out of the band and sent away on the next bus out of town. Thus began his dark side. After all, he had made a very audible contribution to Metallica's early years with his unique guitar style, adding his signature to hits like "Metal Militia," "Jump in the Fire," and "Ride the Lightning." Although he went on to found Megadeth, which became a huge success in its own right, Mustaine held an open grudge against Metallica for decades. What a perfect excuse to devise a decidedly bitter cocktail, based on a glassful of vermouth and Suze.

RUST IN BITTERNESS

INGREDIENTS

- 20 mL Suze
- 20 mL gin
- 20 mL rosso vermouth
- 10 mL lemon juice
- 10 mL crème de pêche
- 100 mL tonic water
- 1 lemon slice (optional)

TOOLS

- Shaker
- Highball glass

DIRECTIONS

1. Pour the Suze, gin, rosso vermouth, lemon juice, and crème de pêche into a shaker. Shake with 5 ice cubes.

2. Strain the cocktail into a highball glass. Add 2 or 3 ice cubes.

3. Add tonic water to fill. Stir.

4. Garnish with a lemon slice, if you choose.

PERFECT PAIRING

This aperitif is perfect with a handful of Kalamata olives.

Marilyn Manson, a popular figure even beyond the sphere of metal music, has a well-known love of absinthe. That was enough to inspire this cocktail based on a spirit with a reputation just as devilish as the controversial shock rocker's.

SCANDAL GALORE

With a stage name that combines two emblematic figures of post–World War II American pop culture (Marilyn Monroe and Charles Manson), Brian Hugh Warner was the ultimate bogeyman for God-fearing America in the 1990s and 2000s. With canceled concerts, endless lawsuits, and allegations of violence, Manson's career was a series of scandals even as his success continued to grow. Manson's detractors even accused him of inciting the youth to extreme violence and depraved acts, an association that recalls absinthe's reputation during its heyday.

Absinthe SUPERSTAR

INGREDIENTS

- 1 bag black tea
- 30 mL absinthe
- 10 mL orgeat syrup
- 20 mL lemon juice
- 3 cucumber slices

TOOLS

- Highball glass or
- Absinthe glass

DIRECTIONS

1. Prepare a cup of black tea, steeping it for only 1 minute.

2. Pour the absinthe, orgeat syrup, and lemon juice into a highball glass or an absinthe glass.

3. Chill the tea with ice cubes.

4. Add cold tea to the glass (about 4 to 5 tablespoons, to taste).

5. Drop 2 ice cubes into the drink, and garnish with the cucumber slices.

In many countries, absinthe has only recently been authorized again after being banned for decades. It was very popular during the nineteenth and early twentieth centuries—nearly 36 million liters of absinthe were produced in France in 1910.

A longside greats like Lemmy Kilmister and Ozzy Osbourne, Dimebag Darrell influenced the course of metal music as few others have. The legendary Pantera guitarist, who died tragically in 2004, has more than earned a place in this book and a tribute cocktail.

Darrell Abbott (his true name) left an indelible mark on metal by perfectly blending the precision of thrash metal, which was already widespread, with the irresistible groove that was just starting to emerge in extreme music genres in the early 1990s. The novel combination stands out within the first seconds of *Vulgar Display of Power*, which Pantera released in 1992. Dimebag played with surgical precision, his guitar sound loud but snappy, embodying a new genre of metal and inspiring a whole generation of guitarists who gave rise several years later to the wave of nu metal that crashed over the planet in the early 2000s. This very "old fashioned" Hail to the King pays tribute to the Texan musician with a quintessentially Southern recipe.

HAIL TO THE KING

INGREDIENTS

- 1 high-quality sugar cube
- 2 dashes Angostura bitters
- 5 mL sparkling water
- 60 mL bourbon
- 1 maraschino cherry
- 1 strip orange zest

TOOLS

- Old fashioned glass

DIRECTIONS

1. Place a sugar cube in an old fashioned glass.

2. Add the Angostura bitters.

3. Pour the sparkling water over the mix to help the sugar dissolve. Stir.

4. Add 1 ice cube. Stir.

5. Add the bourbon and another ice cube, and then stir again.

6. Fill the glass with ice cubes, and garnish with 1 maraschino cherry and a strip of orange zest.

The Old Fashioned Whiskey Cocktail, as it was originally called, is a giant among cocktails. It was first created by James E. Pepper in Kentucky in 1884, and it's incredibly easy to "twist."

A ny metalhead worth their salt knows that the Warlock is the ultimate metal guitar. A legendary instrument deserves a legendary drink!

The Warlock, an iconic guitar model produced by B.C. Rich Guitars, found its first fans among musicians in hard rock and jazz rock bands in the 1970s. But it wasn't until the 1980s, when heavy metal and thrash exploded in popularity, that the model suddenly began to spread like wildfire to concert stages around the world. These days, metal legends like Erik Rutan (Morbid Angel and Cannibal Corpse) and Kerry King (Slayer) are outspoken ambassadors for the brand. Our tribute is a twist on a margarita, in honor of B.C. Rich's California roots.

Warlock

INGREDIENTS

- 50 mL tequila
- 15 mL falernum syrup (recipe: see Feuer Über Alles, page 94)
- 15 mL Cointreau
- 20 mL lime juice
- 1 dash saline solution

TOOLS

- Shaker
- Coupe glass

DIRECTIONS

1. Pour the tequila, falernum syrup, Cointreau, lime juice, and saline solution into a shaker.

2. Shake vigorously with 5 ice cubes.

3. Strain the cocktail into a chilled coupe glass.

SALINE SOLUTION

To make a saline solution, combine 1 tablespoon salt with 1 tablespoon grappa until fully dissolved. Use it sparingly, but 1 or 2 drops of saline solution will improve most cocktails. You can also make it with cognac, Armagnac, tequila, or even mezcal for a smoky flavor.

Wherever you find a blazing sun, desert psychedelics, and a sticky groove, Josh Homme and the Queens of the Stone Age can never be far away. Here's the ultimate recipe for listening to the full Desert Sessions in the blazing heat, with the volume cranked up to 11.

QOTSA, Desert Sessions, Them Crooked Vultures, Eagles of Death Metal, and Kyuss all have one thing in common: Josh Homme. A living legend, he invented desert rock and the famous stoner sound, and he has contributed his magic as a guitar player and music producer to countless projects. His passion is drawing out the sounds of vintage rock during epic jam sessions in the Mojave Desert in California, where he invites musicians from all different backgrounds to play together for days on end, resulting in legendary experimental recordings. We dedicate this twist on a tequila sunrise, the perfect drink for a hot summer day, to Homme's bottomless thirst for creativity.

TEQUILA QUEEN

INGREDIENTS

- 5 mL grenadine syrup
- 5 mL crème de cassis
- 45 mL tequila
- 15 mL Cointreau
- 15 mL lime juice
- 80 mL (⅓ cup) fresh orange juice

TOOLS

- Highball glass
- Shaker

DIRECTIONS

1. Pour the grenadine and crème de cassis into a highball glass. Add 3 ice cubes.

2. Add tequila, Cointreau, lime juice, and orange juice to a shaker.

3. Shake vigorously with 5 ice cubes.

4. Gently strain the cocktail into the glass to create the famous sunrise.

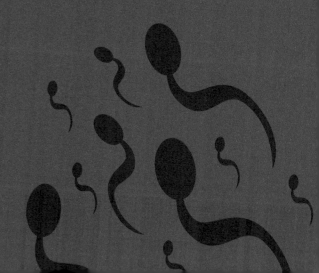

How do you know you're at a metal concert? If the band is playing in front of a wall of black amps with gold trim, your chances of being at a show by a thrash or other metal band are approximately 666 percent.

Marshall, the famous amplifier company, was founded in Britain in 1962 when Pete Townshend, guitarist for the Who, joined forces with Jim Marshall in search of a more powerful sound. By the 1980s, most metal and hard rock bands (including Metallica, Megadeth, Guns N' Roses, and Slayer) would have nothing but the now-legendary JCM800 guitar amps, which helped to shape the predominant metal sound of the decade. Today the British brand has become popular for the massive "walls of sound" these bands would build onstage by stacking their amps, creating an iconic presence for metal fans and musicians alike. Our tribute to the legend is a bronze-colored cocktail based on gin, a quintessentially British spirit.

Wall of Sound

INGREDIENTS

- 50 mL gin
- 20 mL lemon juice
- 15 mL honey syrup (recipe: see Molten Gold, page 92)
- 10 mL fresh orange juice
- 1 teaspoon powdered activated charcoal
- 1 sheet edible gold leaf

TOOLS

- Shaker
- Coupe glass

DIRECTIONS

1. Pour the gin, lemon juice, honey syrup, orange juice, and powdered activated charcoal into a shaker.

2. Shake vigorously with 5 ice cubes.

3. Strain the cocktail into a glass, and watch as it takes on a dark black color from the activated charcoal.

4. Garnish with a small piece of gold leaf.

This drinkable tribute to Alice Cooper smells like the tropical jungles where his infamous snakes love to bask: hot as his leather pants and muggy as a hard rock riff!

Drummer Neal Smith gave Alice Cooper his first snake in 1971. When he got over being scared, the hard rocker quickly saw an opportunity to make the snake part of his persona and even featured one on the cover of his *Killer* album. These days, the vocalist is well known for his many reptile pets. We're just grateful for the excuse to enjoy some tropical flavors with this long cocktail featuring hibiscus syrup.

CALLOUS COOPER

INGREDIENTS

- 50 mL rum
- 15 mL lime juice
- 15 mL hibiscus syrup
- 15 mL banana juice
- 1 dried hibiscus flower

TOOLS

- Shaker
- Coupe glass

DIRECTIONS

1. Pour the rum, lime juice, hibiscus syrup, and banana juice into a shaker.

2. Shake vigorously with 5 ice cubes.

3. Pour the cocktail into a glass, and garnish with the hibiscus flower.

HIBISCUS SYRUP

To make the hibiscus syrup, heat ½ cup water with ½ cup sugar and 1 ounce dried hibiscus flowers until the mixture just starts to simmer; then remove from heat. Stir until the sugar has completely dissolved, strain, and store in the refrigerator.

How could we talk about metal without mentioning its conquering guitar heroes? This special dedication goes out to the most famous one of all, Yngwie Malmsteen, the Swedish prince of the six-string

Lars Johan Yngve Lannerbäck (his real name) was born in Stockholm in 1963. After watching a Jimi Hendrix tribute on TV at age seven, Yngwie decided to become a guitar hero himself. He started playing on an acoustic guitar but switched to electric at the age of nine. When he discovered the work of Italian composer Paganini, it influenced his playing for decades to come. The ultimate symbol of a metal virtuoso, Yngwie has been playing stages around the world ever since, and he remains a role model for millions of metal guitarists. Think he's got fast fingers? You'll be quick as lightening, too, when you mix this drink in a flash!

Guitar HERO

INGREDIENTS

- ⚜ 50 mL gin
- ⚜ 20 mL cherry liqueur
- ⚜ 20 mL lime juice
- ⚜ 10 mL simple syrup
- ⚜ 1 dash Angostura bitters
- ⚜ 1 strip orange zest

TOOLS

- ⚜ Shaker
- ⚜ Coupe glass

DIRECTIONS

① Pour the gin, cherry liqueur, lime juice, simple syrup, and Angostura bitters into a shaker.

② Shake vigorously with 5 ice cubes.

③ Strain the cocktail into a chilled glass.

④ Express a strip of orange zest, and drop it into the cocktail.

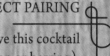

PERFECT PAIRING

As a nod to Yngwie's Swedish roots, serve this cocktail with a platter of smoked fish (like salmon or herring).

We couldn't possibly leave out former Metallica bassist Cliff Burton, who was tragically killed on tour in a bus crash. Cliff was an extremely talented bass player, known for his integrity and admired for his fingerstyle technique, which shaped the sound of the Four Horsemen's early albums.

The best way to remember Cliff and his phenomenal bass playing is to listen to his legendary live solo on "Anesthesia Pulling Teeth" in 1983. For minutes on end, Cliff's bass roars out a series of complex high-pitched motifs alternating with bursts of saturated sound worthy of Metallica's most thrash moments. If we had to narrow down the entire history of metal to just one bass hero, it would be him. Mix up a batch of To Live Is to Die, and share it with your friends over a round of "remember when . . ." RIP Cliff.

to live is to die

SERVES 4

INGREDIENTS

- 200 mL gin
- 50 mL elderflower liqueur
- 50 mL lemon juice
- 50 mL apple juice
- 500 mL tonic water
- 10 cucumber slices plus more for garnishing

TOOLS

- Teapot
- 4 teacups

DIRECTIONS

1. Carefully pour the gin, elderflower liqueur, lemon juice, apple juice, and tonic water into a teapot containing a few ice cubes. Add in the cucumber slices.

2. Stir gently. Set aside for 2 minutes.

3. Pour the cocktail into teacups.

4. Garnish each with a cucumber slice.

5. Settle in with your friends, and enjoy: It's teatime!

PERFECT PAIRING

An almond tea cake is delicious with this soothing beverage.

LEGENDARY SONGS

It's hard to choose just one of the many hits spawned by American band Type O Negative. This cocktail is inspired by Peter Steele's obsession with the color green, although it's named for the song "Black No. 1."

THE GREEN MAN

An 11-minute, 15-second tour de force, "Black No. 1" remains one of the band's most popular songs, showcasing its ability to create dark pop anthems that blend lead guitar choruses with depressing chanted refrains to undeniable effect. Steele's bass snakes insidiously through the opening measures as he murmurs, "She's in love with herself / She likes the dark / On her milk white neck / The Devil's mark." It's hard to imagine a more goth introduction. The cocktail we created is a nod to the green color that saturated all the group's visuals, from their album covers to their stage set bathed in greenish light.

BLACK NUMBER ⊖NE

INGREDIENTS

- 50 mL gin
- 20 mL lime juice
- 10 mL simple syrup
- 1 egg white
- 30 mL sparkling water
- 1 sprig basil

TOOLS

- Shaker
- Old fashioned glass

DIRECTIONS

1. Pour the gin, lime juice, simple syrup, and egg white into the shaker.

2. Dry shake (without ice) vigorously to emulsify.

3. Add 5 ice cubes to the shaker. Shake for another 10 seconds to chill the cocktail.

4. Immediately pour the sparkling water into the shaker.

5. Double strain the cocktail into a chilled glass.

6. Garnish with the sprig of basil.

BARTENDER'S TIP

Many cocktails call for an egg white. To make these recipes properly, you generally need to shake twice: once to emulsify the cocktail (without ice) and again to chill it (with ice). Note that the egg white can be replaced with aquafaba, which is the cooking liquid from chickpeas.

A simple hardcore punk track somehow gives rise to an entire life philosophy? Just another day in the annals of extreme music. This alcohol-free mocktail is our tribute to the Straight Edge movement, which was created exactly like that.

Alongside Perfecto jackets and bullet belts, the early 1980s ushered in a host of bands that borrowed the fast pace of thrash and the violence of punk and then mixed in political messages. This was the birth of the hardcore movement, a close relative to metal. Leading the charge was Minor Threat with its iconic track "Straight Edge." The movement called for abstaining from alcohol, smoking, drugs, and promiscuous sex and promoted a vegan lifestyle. Such an exception to the metal rule deserves its own ginger ale–based recipe!

STRAIGHT X EDGE

INGREDIENTS

- 60 mL freshly squeezed grapefruit juice
- 20 mL lime juice
- 15 mL falernum syrup (recipe: see Feuer Über Alles, page 94)
- 100 mL ginger ale
- 1 strip grapefruit zest
- 1 sprig rosemary

TOOLS

- Large wine glass
- Bar spoon

DIRECTIONS

1) Fill a fancy wine glass with ice cubes. Carefully, one at a time, pour in the grapefruit juice, lime juice, falernum syrup, and ginger ale.

2) Stir with a bar spoon.

3) Drop the grapefruit zest into the glass, and then garnish with a sprig of rosemary.

PERFECT PAIRING

This thirst-quenching mocktail is delicious with homemade hummus.

INGREDIENTS

- 50 mL gin
- 30 mL peppered strawberry purée
- 20 mL lime juice
- 2 sprigs mint
- 100 mL ginger beer
- 1 strawberry

TOOLS

- Shaker
- Highball glass

DIRECTIONS

1. Add the gin, strawberry purée, and lime juice to a shaker. Shake.

2. Rub a glass with fresh mint, and then pour in the shaken cocktail.

3. Add ice cubes and ginger beer to fill the glass. Stir.

4. Garnish with a strawberry and a sprig of mint.

PEPPERED STRAWBERRY PURÉE

To make the peppered strawberry purée: Add ¼ cup sugar, 3½ tablespoons water, 5 chopped strawberries, and 3 to 4 turns of a pepper mill to a saucepan. Cook over low heat until the sugar has completely dissolved. Remove from heat. Stir, strain, and store in the refrigerator for up to a week.

How could we possibly forget Eddie, the iconic mascot of English band Iron Maiden and the face of its top album, *Fear of the Dark*? In honor of the groundbreaking Brits, we've whipped up a cocktail based on a London pub standby.

THE ULTIMATE HEAVY METAL HIT

After all, stout—most commonly, Guinness across the pond—is a type of dark beer, and dark is exactly the base we needed to conjure the same ominous mood Iron Maiden does here. Bruce Dickinson sets a creepy tone from the first verse, singing, "I am a man who walks alone / And when I'm walking a dark road" over a sparse background of guitar picking.

BEER OF THE DARK

INGREDIENTS

- 30 mL rye whiskey
- 10 mL simple syrup
- 2 dashes Angostura bitters
- 60 mL dark beer (preferably with strong coffee notes)
- 1 strip orange zest

TOOLS

- Mixing glass
- Bar spoon
- Old fashioned glass

DIRECTIONS

1. Pour the rye whiskey, simple syrup, and Angostura bitters into a mixing glass filled with ice cubes.

2. Stir with a bar spoon.

3. Pour the cocktail into an old fashioned glass.

4. Top with the cold dark beer.

5. Express a strip of orange zest, and then add it to the glass.

Rye whiskey, a quintessential American spirit, must be distilled from at least 51 percent rye grain.

Australia is known around the world for two things: AC/DC and ginger ale. We've combined them into a refreshing beverage, perfect for drinking while you sing along to the band's biggest hit, "Highway to Hell."

Angus Young's group has written plenty of powerful music, but if we had to pick just one to send into space to explain hard rock to any aliens out there, it would be "Highway to Hell," hands down. With its driving beat, thunderous guitar riffs, and unrelenting chorus, this hit track from the band's eponymous fifth album, released in 1979, embodies the purest AC/DC sound and features Bon Scott's magnetic vocal performance. Mix up this cocktail and lift your glass while you belt out the hellish refrain!

HIGHWAY TO GINGER ALE

INGREDIENTS

- 50 mL gin
- 20 mL Pimm's
- 20 mL lime juice
- 100 mL ginger ale
- 1 lime wedge
- 1 sprig mint

TOOLS

- Mule mug

DIRECTIONS

1. Fill a mule mug with ice cubes, and then carefully pour in the gin, Pimm's, lime juice, and ginger ale, one at a time.

2. Stir.

3. Garnish with the lime wedge and mint.

What's the difference between ginger beer and ginger ale?
Ginger beer is a soda made from fermented ginger with yeast and lemon.
Ginger ale, meanwhile, is a ginger-flavored carbonated beverage.

We're off to Italy with this cocktail inspired by "The Godfather," the opening track to *The Director's Cut* by Fantômas, the supergroup featuring vocalist Mike Patton.

Fantômas's second album, released in 2001, is a compilation of iconic movie themes spiced up with experimental metal sounds and a roller coaster of a vocal performance by Patton, who's also the lead vocalist for Faith No More. On the album, the band has completely deconstructed the instrumental theme originally composed by Nino Rota for *The Godfather*, piecing together sudden explosions of grind with adventurous smooth jazz sections. Join us in southern Italy to toast their masterpiece with this recipe featuring Campari and Cynar.

Don Patton

INGREDIENTS

- ❦ 20 mL gin
- ❦ 20 mL Campari
- ❦ 20 mL Cynar
- ❦ 20 mL rosso vermouth
- ❦ 1 strip orange zest

TOOLS

- ❦ Mixing glass
- ❦ Old fashioned glass

DIRECTIONS

1. Pour the gin, Campari, Cynar, and rosso vermouth into a mixing glass.

2. Stir.

3. Strain the cocktail into an old fashioned glass filled with ice cubes.

4. Express a strip of orange zest, and then add it to the glass.

PERFECT PAIRING

A plate of marinated anchovy fillets and a few artichokes in oil is delicious with this cocktail.

W hat could be more appropriate than drinking a shooter while listening to the shortest song in the entire history of music?

We owe the track, which lasts precisely 1.316 seconds, to English grindcore band Napalm Death, which released it in 1987 on its first album, simply titled *Scum*. The extreeeeeeeeemely short piece was officially recognized by the *Guinness Book of World Records* as the shortest recorded song in the world. We challenge you to perform it at your next karaoke night, growling out "You suffer—but why?" alongside Nicholas Bullen, the band's vocalist at the time. Consider this shooter our ovation!

you suffer.

INGREDIENTS

- ❦ 15 mL Cointreau
- ❦ 15 mL Adriatico amaretto
- ❦ 15 mL pineapple juice

TOOLS

- ❦ Shot glass

DIRECTIONS

Pour the Cointreau, Adriatico amaretto, and pineapple juice into a chilled shot glass, and drink as fast as possible!

ICONIC ALBUMS AND COVER ART

Because we all need to revisit our childhood from time to time, we've created this updated milkshake to sip while listening to (for ultimate regression) Limp Bizkit's cult classic, *Chocolate Starfish and the Hot Dog Flavored Water*. Get out your baggy jeans.

It's the year 2000, and a new wave is taking over the world of metal. Goodbye, leather and bullet belts; hello, baseball caps, baggy jeans, and streetwear. The nu metal revolution is here, and kids around the world are lining up to join in. Although Korn appeared to be the uncontested leader at the start of this largely US-driven movement, it was Limp Bizkit that eventually emerged as the most emblematic band of the era, with its potent mix of energy, incredibly cheesy tracks, and juvenile refrains. Come back to the future with our Nu Milkshake, perfectly calibrated for sitting around in a sweatsuit in the late afternoon.

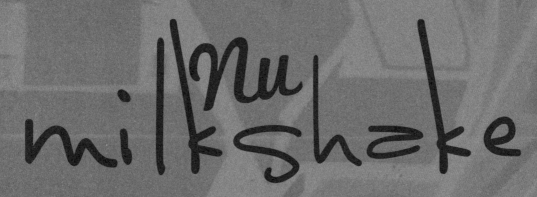

nu milkshake

INGREDIENTS

- 1 scoop chocolate ice cream
- 50 mL Baileys
- 10 mL Chartreuse Verte
- Whipped cream
- Chocolate syrup
- 1 large homemade cookie

TOOLS

- Blender
- Fountain glass

DIRECTIONS

1. Blend together the ice cream, Baileys, and Chartreuse Verte.

2. Pour the Nu Milkshake into a fountain glass.

3. Garnish with the whipped cream, chocolate syrup, and homemade cookie.

This bizarre song, the title track of Mortician's cult classic EP, has an equally bizarre sound, creating an extreme gore aesthetic that is instantly recognizable—just like this smoked cocktail, which is sure to awaken your inner zombie!

Z MOVIES AND SERIAL MASSACRES

You can't call yourself a real metalhead if you've never listened to Mortician. Give up just 2 minutes and 48 seconds of your existence to listen to "Zombie Apocalypse," and you'll see what we mean. With samples from Z movies, wildly detuned guitars, robotic drum machine beats, and a sub-bass growl, Mortician has become an icon by cranking every dial of death grind to the extreme—even the grotesque. In the process, the group has created a ludicrous, lumbering style that borders on the comical. Mix up this cocktail on the night of a full moon while praying to the Devil, and fire up your chain saw . . .

ZOMBIE APOCALYPSE

INGREDIENTS

- 1 stick cinnamon
- 30 mL Cuban rum
- 30 mL rhum agricole
- 20 mL lime juice
- 15 mL amaretto
- 5 mL anise-flavored liqueur
- 40 mL pineapple juice
- 10 mL grapefruit juice
- 1 pineapple leaf
- 1 sprig mint

TOOLS

- Highball glass
- Shaker

DIRECTIONS

1. Light a stick of cinnamon on fire, and then snuff it out by placing the highball glass upside down over the stick. Let the glass absorb the smoke flavor.

2. Pour the Cuban rum, rhum Agricole, lime juice, amaretto, anise-flavored liqueur, pineapple juice, and grapefruit juice into a shaker.

3. Shake vigorously with 5 ice cubes.

4. Turn the glass right side up, and strain the cocktail into it.

5. Add enough crushed ice to fill the glass, and then garnish with the pineapple leaf and mint sprig.

Tiki drinks were invented by Texan bartender Donn Beach, who loved to travel. The erstwhile bootlegger opened a South Pacific–themed restaurant called Don the Beachcomber after the end of Prohibition, where he served cocktails featuring fruit juice and honey.

Blue as the ocean with the foam of crashing waves, the Blood & Thunder was inspired by *Leviathan*, the album that launched Mastodon's career. Let's dive right in!

This second recording by Troy Sanders's band is a concept album loosely based on Herman Melville's *Moby Dick*. Just like the album's cover art, which depicts the titanic clash between an enormous whale and a ship in a raging sea, the song punctuates controlled sludge with a maelstrom of epic power stoner melodies, a perfect musical incarnation of the nautical saga. The album was unanimously hailed by critics and was named Best Alternative Metal Album by Metal Storm in 2004.

BLOOD & THUNDER

INGREDIENTS

- 45 mL gin
- 20 mL curaçao
- 20 mL lemon juice
- 10 mL simple syrup
- 1 egg white (or 15 mL aquafaba)
- 1 strip lemon zest

TOOLS

- Shaker
- Coupe glass

DIRECTIONS

1. Pour the gin, curaçao, lemon juice, simple syrup, and egg white (or aquafaba) into a shaker

2. Dry shake (without ice) vigorously to emulsify.

3. Add 5 ice cubes to the shaker. Shake for another 10 seconds to chill the cocktail.

4. Immediately strain the cocktail into a chilled coupe glass.

5. Express a strip of lemon zest, and then add it to the glass.

Our Blood & Thunder is based on the White Lady, one of several classic cocktails invented by legendary bartender Harry MacElhone, who bought Harry's New York Bar in Paris in 1923. His original recipe called for crème de menthe, but MacElhone soon swapped it out for gin and adjusted the proportions of triple sec and lemon juice. His new version of the White Lady is now served at bars around the world.

Considered one of the founding albums of modern metal, *Burn My Eyes* forms a bridge between old-school, late-1980s thrash and a more modern style of composition that ultimately inspired an entire generation of metalheads to lead the nu metal charge of the 2000s.

When it landed in 1994, this record stirred up a small revolution on the metal scene. With thrash stuck in a rut and death metal hitting its stride, Machine Head shook things up by adding just enough of a modern groove to its metal to create the beginnings of a new genre. Just take a listen to the opening track, "Davidian," which finds its inspiration somewhere between Pantera's power/thrash and Panzer Division's double bass drum sound. In short, it was a breath of fresh air—just like our recipe, which adds a splash of modernity to a traditional drink.

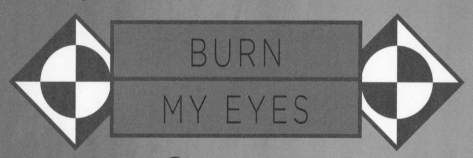

BURN MY EYES

INGREDIENTS

- 50 mL rum
- 15 mL vanilla syrup
- 20 mL lime juice
- 40 mL mango juice
- 40 mL passion fruit juice
- 1 sprig mint
- ½ fresh passion fruit

TOOLS

- Highball glass
- Shaker

DIRECTIONS

1. Pour the rum, vanilla syrup, lime juice, mango juice, and passion fruit juice into a shaker.

2. Shake vigorously with 5 ice cubes.

3. Strain the cocktail into a chilled highball glass.

4. Add crushed ice to fill.

5. Garnish with a sprig of mint and half a fresh passion fruit.

The Porn Star Martini, which inspired this cocktail, was invented in 2002 by Douglas Ankrah and is traditionally served with a shot of champagne. It's now a modern classic.

With its somber, musty, unsettling mood and dark romanticism, King Diamond's second album, *Abigail*, has all the hallmarks of a ghost story. It's easy to imagine the story taking place in an old Louisiana mansion.

The nine-track concept album opens with an atmospheric buildup of gothic chords before giving way to a cavalcade of heavy metal led by the high-pitched voice of King Diamond, the dark priest of this macabre metal mass. He tells the tragic tale of a young couple who ignore the supernatural warnings of seven mysterious horsemen. The chilling story, which conjures the baroque ambiance of a Louisiana bayou peopled with the ghosts of Southern plantations, was our inspiration for this recipe.

La Louisiane

INGREDIENTS

- 40 mL rye whiskey
- 30 mL vermouth
- 20 mL Bénédictine
- 2 dashes Peychaud's bitters
- Maraschino cherries

TOOLS

- Shaker
- Coupe glass

DIRECTIONS

1. Pour the rye whiskey, vermouth, Bénédictine, and Peychaud's bitters into a shaker.

2. Shake vigorously with 5 ice cubes for 9 seconds.

3. Strain the cocktail into a coupe glass.

4. Garnish with a small skewer of maraschino cherries.

PERFECT PAIRING

Serve with Cajun pork ribs, obviously!

South America is bursting with exciting flavors, pungent ingredients, rare spices, and tastes that have always piqued the curiosity of mixologists. The lush forests of Brazil are no exception. They served up plenty of inspiration for this Caipultura, a cocktail dedicated to the most famous Brazilian band in the metal world: Sepultura.

THE CALL OF THE WILD

The Cavalera brothers' group first burst onto the metal stage with *Chaos A.D.*, like a splash of icy water in the face for a scene struggling to reconcile thrash-death violence with urban groove. But it was *Roots* that left a unique mark on extreme music by injecting a solid dose of traditional sound. That was reason enough for us to dedicate a cocktail to Sepultura. We've mixed mango juice, from the ultimate tropical fruit, with cachaça, Brazil's most popular spirit, which is distilled from sugarcane.

CAIPULTURA

DIRECTIONS

1. Quarter the half-lime, and add to the glass along with the brown sugar and chili pepper syrup.

2. Muddle.

3. Pour in the cachaça and mango juice.

4. Add crushed ice to fill the glass.

5. Stir well.

INGREDIENTS

- ½ lime
- 1 teaspoon brown sugar
- 10 mL chile pepper syrup
- 50 mL cachaça
- 50 mL mango juice
- Crushed ice

TOOLS

- Old fashioned glass
- Muddler

CHILE PEPPER SYRUP

To make your own chile pepper syrup, place 5 bird's eye chiles and 1 cup water in a small saucepan over low heat. Add 1 cup sugar, and stir until it's dissolved. Remove from heat, strain, and store in the refrigerator for up to 2 months.

I n this twist on the famous Bramble invented by Dick Bradsell in 1984, the gin is replaced with Irish whiskey and blackberry, a fruit whose red-staining juice certainly would have excited the imagination of Countess Báthory, the heroine of a concept album by English vampire band Cradle of Filth.

Cradle of Filth launched its career with several iconic albums, including *Cruelty and the Beast*, which follows the life of Countess Elizabeth Báthory. A nefarious character, she is rumored to have terrorized the countryside surrounding her home in sixteenth-century Hungary. Known as the Blood Countess, she is considered one of the most infamous murderers of Hungarian and Slovak history, accused of having killed many girls and young women. This quintessential gothic album refers to the legend that the countess used to bathe in the blood of her victims in order to remain young and beautiful.

BÁTHORY BRAMBLE

INGREDIENTS

- 50 mL Irish whiskey
- 20 mL lemon juice, strained
- 15 mL simple syrup
- 1 fresh blackberry
- 1 lemon, for zesting
- 10 mL crème de mûre

TOOLS

- Old fashioned glass
- Shaker

DIRECTIONS

1. Add the whiskey, lemon juice, and simple syrup to a shaker.

2. Shake with 5 ice cubes.

3. Strain the cocktail into a chilled old fashioned glass.

4. Add a pile of crushed ice, and place the fresh blackberry on top.

5. Peel a strip of lemon zest directly over the glass to capture the essential oils.

6. Pour the crème de mûre over the cocktail, like a trail of hot blood melting a thick layer of snow.

The history of metal is studded with appalling cover art. The cult classic cover of *Butchered at Birth*, by American band Cannibal Corpse, will probably remain one of the genre's most controversial. We considered it fitting inspiration for this recipe, carefully calibrated to awaken your inner butcher.

Having the cover art for an album rejected by its own record label is unquestionably one of Cannibal Corpse's most emblematic exploits. In 1991, George Fisher and his brutal death metal band had just finished mixing their second long-format album at Morrisound Studio in Florida. The music was a concentrated dose of pure violence, driven by George's voiceless growls and evoking every gory theme imaginable: vivisection, gutting, amputation, and every stage of decomposition. For its artwork, the band chose an appropriate illustration depicting two corpses in butcher outfits eviscerating a body, surrounded by a mess of blood and entrails. Yum! By way of tribute, we created a cocktail strong enough to wake the dead.

CANNIBAL REVIVER

INGREDIENTS

- Absinthe, for rinsing the glass
- 25 mL gin
- 25 mL dessert wine
- 25 mL Cointreau
- 25 mL lemon juice
- 1 dash Peychaud's bitters (optional)

TOOLS

- Coupe glass
- Shaker

DIRECTIONS

1. Rinse the coupe glass with a bit of absinthe; then discard the absinthe.

2. Pour the gin, dessert wine, Cointreau, and lemon juice into a shaker. Shake with 5 ice cubes.

3. Strain the cocktail into the glass.

4. If you have it, add a dash of Peychaud's bitters.

PERFECT PAIRING

Fresh red meat, of course! Serve the Cannibal Reviver with beef carpaccio and hot sauce.

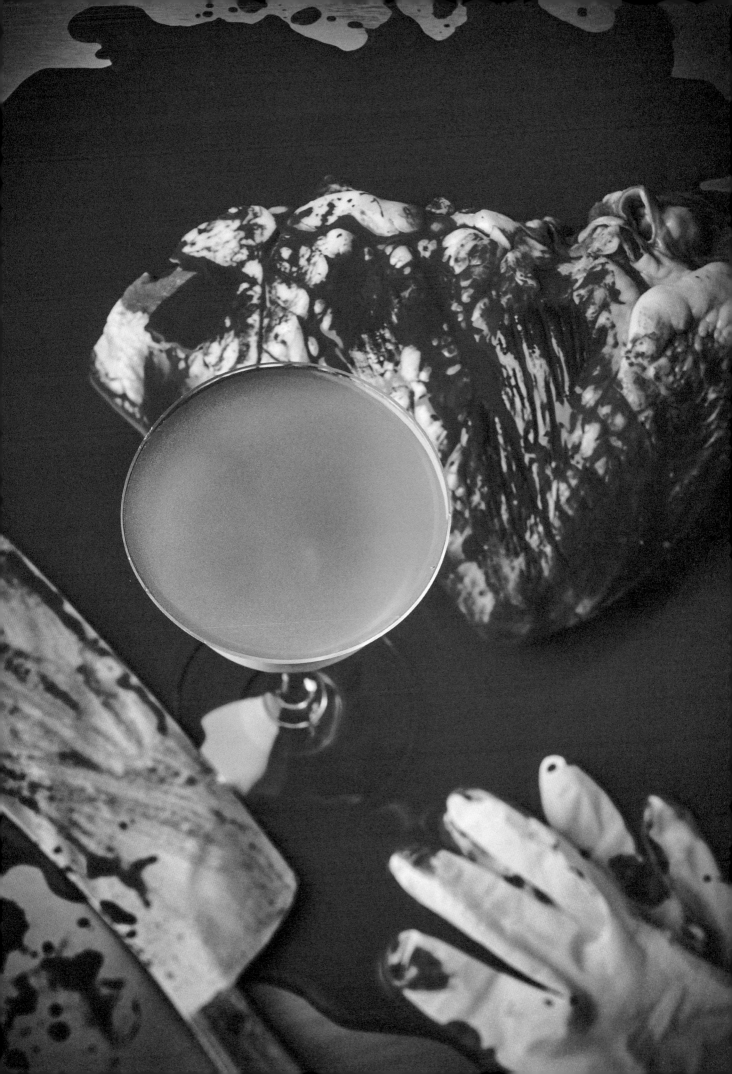

Red like the cover of the band's first album and spirited as James Hetfield's guitar playing, Drink 'Em All is the perfect combination of the hot blood of Metallica's young upstarts and the blazing sun that grows the main ingredients for this fiery cocktail.

When Lars Ulrich and James Hetfield first met in the early 1980s, they could hardly have imagined the career they were about to embark on. Their collaboration and shared passion for the New Wave of British Heavy Metal gave rise to one of the decade's most exciting bands, a pioneer of thrash metal. Although Lars is Danish, Metallica's early career and the composition of the band's first album, *Kill 'Em All*, were heavily influenced by the culture of the American Southwest. The two got their start in Los Angeles; the band then traveled the southwestern states on its first tour, chose San Francisco as home base, and built up substantial audiences in Texas and New Mexico, which are right next door to Mexico—the birthplace of mezcal!

DRINK'EM ALL

INGREDIENTS

- 45 mL mezcal
- 25 mL lime juice
- 10 mL crème de cassis
- 15 mL simple syrup
- 90 mL ginger beer
- 1 blood orange round or wedge

TOOLS

- Highball glass
- Bar spoon

DIRECTIONS

1. Pour the mezcal, lime juice, crème de cassis, and simple syrup into a chilled highball glass. Stir.

2. Add 5 ice cubes to the glass to fill, and then pour in the ginger beer.

3. Give the drink a single stir with the bar spoon.

4. Garnish with a round or wedge of blood orange.

BARTENDER'S TIP

Try it with other crème liqueurs for different flavors.

LIVE SHOWS

One band absolutely has to show up in this book: Manowar. To them, we dedicate this gilded cocktail. A good glug of honey makes it look like molten gold, and the bold blend of bourbon and peated whiskey will grow hair on your chest. Guess we're the bosses now!

Pompous, bombastic, loutish, ear-shatteringly loud, painfully literal, and yet idolized like almost no other band, Manowar is an icon on the metal scene and still venerated by millions of fans around the globe. The band, founded by Joey DeMaio, holds several records, including the longest metal concert (they played 40 songs to a crowd of 20,000 people for 5 hours and 10 minutes) and loudest concert (recorded at 129.5 dB during a show in Hanover in 1994). Our Molten Gold, a twist on the famous cocktail called Penicillin, captures the fiery color and smoky, manly scent of peated whiskey, along with a subtle, wild acidity from ginger and lemon. Crank up the volume to max, and grab your shaker!

MOLTEN GOLD

DIRECTIONS

1. Using a muddler, smash the ginger in the bottom of the shaker. Pour in the bourbon, honey syrup, and lemon juice.

2. Shake vigorously.

3. Empty the cocktail into an old fashioned glass filled with ice cubes.

4. Pour the whiskey over the cocktail.

5. Garnish with a lemon slice.

INGREDIENTS

- 1 slice fresh ginger
- 40 mL bourbon
- 10 mL honey syrup
- 20 mL lemon juice
- 10 mL peated whiskey
- 1 slice lemon

TOOLS

- Muddler
- Shaker
- Old fashioned glass

HONEY SYRUP

To make honey syrup, combine ⅔ cup honey with 1 cup hot water in a container, and stir until the honey has completely dissolved. Store for up to 1 month in the refrigerator.

Any tribute to Rammstein clearly has to include the signature that makes the band's live shows so insane: fire. We think the pyrotechnics of this tiki-inspired cocktail are pretty lit.

During a span of nearly 30 years, Rammstein has been a force on the global metal scene, despite the group's German lyrics in a genre dominated by English. The band broke through the language barrier in 1997 with the release of *Sehnsucht* and won a large fan base at a time when electronic music was beginning to creep into the heavy sound of metal guitars. The hit song "Du Hast" became a number one single worldwide and a high point of Rammstein's epic concerts, which feature spectacular pyrotechnics. Rammstein is now a supergroup, and we designed this super-cocktail to be just as impressive as the group's stage show.

FEUER ÜBER ALLES

INGREDIENTS

- 40 mL rum
- 20 mL lime juice
- 15 mL falernum syrup
- 15 mL Cointreau
- 60 mL pineapple juice
- 1 pineapple slice
- 1 lime wedge
- 10 mL rhum agricole (50 percent ABV)
- Ground cinnamon

TOOLS

- Shaker
- Highball glass
- Straw

DIRECTIONS

1. Pour the rum, lime juice, falernum syrup, Cointreau, and pineapple juice into the shaker. Shake.

2. Empty the contents of the shaker into the highball glass, and then fill to the top with crushed ice.

3. Garnish with the straw and pineapple slice.

4. Soak the lime wedge in the rhum agricole, place it on top of the cocktail, and light it on fire.

5. Make sparks by throwing ground cinnamon over the flaming drink while chanting "Du Hast!"

FALERNUM SYRUP

It's easy to make a good falernum syrup yourself. Pour 2 cups sugar into a saucepan with 1⅔ cups almond milk. Add 1 ounce minced fresh ginger, 2 cloves, 1 cinnamon stick, and 1 split vanilla bean. Cook on low heat, stirring, until the sugar is dissolved. Remove from heat, and let cool; then strain into a bottle. Store in the refrigerator for up to 2 weeks.

W couldn't possibly fail to mention one of the biggest congregations of metal fans in Europe, Hellfest. No self-respecting metalhead would miss out on this annual summer ritual, so we've created a drink you can bring along and share with your friends.

Hellfest is a bit like the World Cup for metalheads: If you've never been, you've basically failed at life. With an all-star lineup, stage sets worthy of a George Lucas film (but a bit heavy on the thrash), and insane ambiance, the festival has become a rite of passage for international bands in Europe. We won't attempt to list every one of the metal superstars who have appeared onstage in Clisson, France. We'd rather you spend your time mixing up this cocktail made with Muscadet (a must, if you're going to be in the Loire Valley) that you can pass around the campfire at next summer's festival.

MUSCADEATH

INGREDIENTS

- 1 bottle Muscadet
- 100 mL Suze
- 200 mL Cointreau
- 50 mL lime juice
- 1 orange
- 1 lime
- 5 strawberries
- 1 L ginger ale
- 2 sprigs mint

TOOLS

- Large mixing bowl or pitcher

DIRECTIONS

1. Pour the wine, Suze, Cointreau, and lime juice into the bowl.

2. Cut the orange, lime, and strawberries into pieces, and add them to the mixture.

3. Refrigerate until ready to serve.

4. Just before serving, add the ginger ale, mint, and some ice cubes.

5. Stir.

LEGENDARY BANDS

Behemoth is the ultimate black metal group, broadly popular and the leader of Poland's very active extreme music scene. This is our tribute to Nergal and his horde, who hail from the birthplace of vodka.

Dark, bombastic, and satanic down to the tips of their black fingernails, Behemoth embodies the music of a metal genre fascinated with occult imagery and the figure of the Devil. Behemoth was formed in 1991 and has appeared on festival stages around the world, gradually building its image as a leader on the Polish scene with lyrics that refer to the works of Aleister Crowley, John Milton, and William Blake. With corpse paint, upside-down crosses, and plenty of studded leather, they look the part of a black metal band. They also sound like one, combining symphonic elements with their death and thrash roots and following their uncompromising leader, Nergal, who practically came back from the dead after surviving a serious case of leukemia. We're celebrating his miraculous recovery with an infernally black cocktail that combines vodka (Polish, of course) with strong espresso.

the satanist

INGREDIENTS

- 45 mL Polish vodka
- 40 mL espresso
- 20 mL Algebra Coffee Liqueur
- 10 mL simple syrup or flavored syrup (vanilla, caramel, coconut)
- 3 coffee beans

TOOLS

- Shaker
- Coupe glass

DIRECTIONS

1. Add the vodka, espresso, coffee liqueur, and simple syrup to a shaker.

2. Shake vigorously for 10 seconds with 5 ice cubes.

3. Strain the cocktail into a coupe glass.

4. Garnish with 3 coffee beans.

Polish vodka is an alcohol made entirely in Poland from traditional ingredients (potatoes, barley, rye, wheat, triticale) that are grown or manufactured locally, and bottled in Poland. It must be a minimum of 37.5 percent ABV and cannot have any additives apart from water.

If there were room for only one French band on the metal scene, it would have to be Gojira, whose remarkable discography has paved the path to global success. As Frenchmen ourselves, we couldn't resist toasting our fellow countrymen with a cocktail of quintessentially French ingredients.

A FAMILY AFFAIR

The story of Gojira begins with the Duplantier brothers: Joe, the vocalist and guitarist, and Mario, the drummer. As young teenagers, the two brothers decided to form their own band under the name Godzilla. The original duo played a blend of thrash and death metal that made for surprisingly good music, enough to have them opening for acts like Cannibal Corpse, Impaled Nazarene, and Immortal. In 2001, the band changed its name to Gojira and released its first album, *Terra Incognita*. It seemed only fitting to celebrate France's champions on the global metal stage with a cocktail made of 100 percent French liqueurs, like Armagnac and Cointreau, mixed with a syrup made with kiwi, a fruit proudly grown along the Adour River that runs through the Duplantiers' home region of Landes.

duplantier

INGREDIENTS

- 45 mL Armagnac
- 25 mL Cointreau
- 15 mL lemon juice
- 10 mL kiwi syrup
- 1 strip lemon zest

TOOLS

- Shaker
- Coupe glass

DIRECTIONS

1. Pour the Armagnac, Cointreau, lemon juice, and kiwi syrup into a shaker. Shake.

2. Transfer the cocktail to a coupe glass.

3. Express a strip of lemon zest, and then add it to the glass.

KIWI SYRUP

To make a good kiwi syrup, you need ½ cup sugar, ½ cup water, and 1 kiwi. Blend together all the ingredients, and store in the refrigerator for up to a week.

P

ull on your leather biker cap and fingerless gloves, and rev up your Harley: It's time to go full metal with this twist on the famous Mint Julep, reinvented as a tribute to one of the biggest New Wave of British Heavy Metal (NWOBHM) bands, Judas Priest.

The band was formed in the mid-1970s and made its mark on the history of the genre by incarnating an extreme heavy metal image to a soundtrack of molten-hot riffs that conjure a biker gang dressed head to toe in studded leather. Longtime vocalist Rob Halford's impressive vocal abilities were responsible for much of the group's unique musical signature. The album *British Steel*, released in spring 1980, swept the band to popularity while laying the foundation for an entire genre, the New Wave of British Heavy Metal. It featured short songs, rhythms perfect for roaring up the highway in a pack, stadium chants, and soaring vocals led by Halford, who would pull onto stage shirtless on a Harley and rev its engine, pumping his fist. The whole effect was a breath of fresh air on the metal scene at the time—an icy wind as cold as steel, much like this cocktail derived from the classic Mint Julep.

Mint judas

INGREDIENTS

- 60 mL bourbon
- 10 mL crème de pêche
- 10 mL simple syrup
- 2 dashes Angostura bitters
- 2 sprigs mint
- 20 mL sparkling water

TOOLS

- Shaker
- Julep cup
- Straw

DIRECTIONS

1. Pour the bourbon, crème de pêche, simple syrup, and Angostura bitters into a shaker. Shake with 5 ice cubes.

2. Double strain the cocktail into a julep cup.

3. Add a few mint leaves. Fill the glass with crushed ice. Pour in the sparkling water, and stir.

4. Garnish with a sprig of mint, and then add a straw.

The Mint Julep, which James Bond drank in *Goldfinger*, was invented in the South in the early 1800s and has been made popular by the Kentucky Derby, a famous horse race where the drink is traditionally served.

This bright blue cocktail, named for the second album by Norwegian band Enslaved, pays tribute to the Viking culture that arose from the deep Scandinavian fjords. *Skol!*

Enslaved has been proudly proclaiming its Viking roots for more than 27 years while constantly growing and evolving its varied and exciting discography. Although the band's original sound was decidedly black metal, its musical reach has now broadened into a style that's dark and sometimes complex—bordering on progressive—but still focused on the thrilling sagas of Norse mythology. A band that can stay true to one theme throughout such a long career deserves a cocktail as cold as the Scandinavian snow and as blue as the waters that gave birth to the fascinating Viking civilization.

DIRECTIONS

1. Add the vodka, curaçao, lime juice, and simple syrup to a blender along with 3 ice cubes.

2. Blend for 40 seconds.

3. Pour into a chilled coupe glass.

4. Make an offering to Odin, and enjoy.

INGREDIENTS

- 60 mL vodka
- 30 mL curaçao
- 20 mL lime juice
- 20 mL simple syrup

TOOLS

- Blender
- Coupe glass

BARTENDER'S TIP

If you don't have a blender, pour all the ingredients into a container with 2 tablespoons of water. Leave the container in the freezer, stirring regularly with a fork, for 24 hours before serving.

It's not uncommon for brands to invite popular metal bands to endorse a product. In this case, we've created a cocktail that features the iconic digestif Jägermeister to celebrate the greatest thrash band of all time: Slayer.

THE BEST OF THE BEST

Even if you stick to bare facts, it's impossible to talk about Slayer and not pile on the compliments. The band has had a foundational impact on extreme music: It was the first to play so fast, the first to shock the world with its emblematic Satanic album covers, and the first to sing such provocatively explicit lyrics. To commemorate the legendary band's legacy, Jägermeister released just 500 limited edition Slayer bottles to coincide with the band's final performance. Lead guitarist Kerry King said, "We've had some good times with Jägermeister through the years." Now it's your turn. We've combined the digestif with the deep dark of crème de cassis for a cocktail straight from the abyss.

Slayermeister

INGREDIENTS

- 40 mL Jägermeister
- 10 mL simple syrup
- 10 mL crème de cassis
- 15 mL lemon juice
- 1 strip lemon zest

TOOLS

- Shaker
- Coupe glass

DIRECTIONS

1. Pour the Jägermeister, simple syrup, crème de cassis, and lemon juice into a shaker with 5 ice cubes.

2. Shake vigorously.

3. Strain the cocktail into a coupe glass.

4. Express a strip of lemon zest, and then add it to the glass.

, the best-known French metal band. The group's parody album *Objectif: Thunes* struck us as the perfect jumping-off point for this cocktail, which features ingredients as stereotypically French as a beret and a baguette.

The Nantes-based band has been a fixture on the French metal scene for more than twenty years, playing its own blend of grind-heavy-thrash-death-power—with a side of cotillion—as it spoofs world-famous acts. The cartoon-loving crew brilliantly parodies the dark and often humorless aspects of the metal scene, with songs that send up Rammstein ("Kammthaar") and heavy metal clichés ("Evier Metal"), and even an effective mash-up of Gojira vs. Calogero on a hilarious track titled "Calogira." Set out some whoopie cushions, and get ready to mix up a cocktail that's truly out there.

OBJECTIF:
PRUNES

INGREDIENTS

- 5 mL Cointreau
- 5 mL simple syrup
- 10 mL Muscadet
- 20 mL plum liqueur

TOOLS

- Shot glass

DIRECTIONS

Pour the Cointreau, simple syrup, Muscadet, and plum liqueur into a chilled shot glass, and serve.

I n the metal galaxy, Voivod and its style of thrash, which combines sci-fi with almost progressive structures, is a bit of a UFO. So is this cocktail based on rye whiskey, the same type historically produced in Canada.

Voivod was formed in Quebec in the early 1980s and holds a special place on the extreme music scene. Although the band's beginnings were marked by the thrash wave that emerged at the time, founding guitarist Denis d'Amour and company quickly embraced a more progressive style of composition and developed music reflecting the band's own unique world, which is heavily influenced by science fiction themes. Voivod has a very oddball reputation on the thrash scene, so we're celebrating it with a quirky recipe based on rye whiskey, a drink that also hails from North America.

INGREDIENTS

- 50 mL rye whiskey
- 100 mL ginger ale
- 1 lime wedge

TOOLS

- Highball glass

DIRECTIONS

1. Fill a highball glass with ice cubes.

2. Pour in the rye whiskey. Add the ginger ale.

3. Squeeze the lime wedge over the cocktail, and then add it to the glass.

PERFECT PAIRING

This ultra-refreshing cocktail is perfect to enjoy with friends alongside a plate of cookies for munching.

INGREDIENTS INDEX

METAL INDEX

ACKNOWLEDGMENTS

FABIEN

I'd like to thank everyone who made this book possible and everyone who helped me become the bartender I am today—above all, my entire family and my close friends. Thank you to my colleagues, my coworkers, and everyone I've met on either side of a bar. Thank you to my staff and everyone who's worked alongside me. Thank you to my partners and to Marc for letting me work on this book. A big thank-you to Yves Cosentino for sharing your knowledge. Thank you to La Nef D Fous and the entire team at the Binic Folks Blues Festival. Thank you to all our patrons at Le Bistrot de la Poste, who put us to the test every day and drive us to keep improving! Most of all, thank you to my wife, Élodie, and my children, Maïlan and Ines, for their support, their patience, and the energy they give me. Thank you very much to The Nice Company for the clear ice and to Jägermeister and Sailor Jerry for the support.

MARC

I'd like to thank my family, my friends, Hachette Heroes for their confidence, and Antoine for his loyalty. Thank you to Fabien for agreeing to help write this book. Thank you to all my old friends who tried my early cocktails, the Marduk and the Jah Breuvage. Thank you to the entire Club team at Le Bistrot de la Poste. And finally and most important, thank you for buying this book!

NICOLAS

A big thank-you to Lucie and the entire Hachette team.
A big thank-you to Fabien for his insane cocktails and to Marc for his metal knowledge!
A big thank-you to Mélanie for her unfailing professionalism and ability to get the job done!

PO Box 3088
San Rafael, CA 94912
www.insighteditions.com

Find us on Facebook: www.facebook.com/InsightEditions
Follow us on Twitter: @insighteditions
Follow us on Instagram: @insighteditions

© 2022, Hachette Livre (Hachette Pratique)
58 Rue Jean Bleuzen – 92178 Vanves Cedex, France

ISBN: 979-8-88663-386-3

Publisher: Raoul Goff
VP, Co-Publisher: Vanessa Lopez
VP, Creative: Chrissy Kwasnik
VP, Manufacturing: Alix Nicholaeff
VP, Group Managing Editor: Vicki Jaeger
Publishing Director: Jamie Thompson
Design Manager: Megan Sinead-Harris
Editor: Jennifer Pellman
Editorial Assistant: Jeff Chiarelli
Managing Editor: Maria Spano
Senior Production Manager: Deena Hashem
Senior Production Manager, Subsidiary Rights: Lina s Palma-Temena
English Translation by Lisa Molle Troyer

Insight Editions, in association with Roots of Peace, will plant two trees for each tree used in the manufacturing of this book. Roots of Peace is an internationally renowned humanitarian organization dedicated to eradicating land mines worldwide and converting war-torn lands into productive farms and wildlife habitats. Roots of Peace will plant two million fruit and nut trees in Afghanistan and provide farmers there with the skills and support necessary for sustainable land use.

Manufactured in China by Insight Editions

10 9 8 7 6 5 4 3 2 1